Linking art to the world around us

artyfacts
Weather

Abbey
Children's
Books

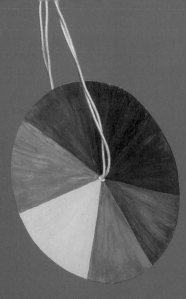

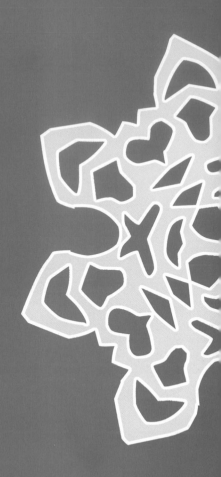

CONCEPT

Publisher: Felicia Law
Design: Tracy Carrington
Editorial Planning: Karen Foster
Research and Development: Gerry Bailey, Alec Edgington

PROJECT DEVELOPMENT

Project Director: Karen Foster
Editors: Claire Sipi, Hazel Songhurst, Samantha Sweeney
Design Director: Tracy Carrington
Design Manager: Flora Awolaja
Design and DTP: Claire Penny, Paul Montague, James Thompson, Mark Dempsey
Photo and Art Editor: Andrea Sadler
Illustrator: Jan Smith
Model Artist: Sophie Dean
Further models: Sue Partington, Abigail Dean
Digital Workflow: Edward MacDermott
Production: Victoria Grimsell, Christina Brown
Scanning: Acumen Colour Ltd

Published by Abbey Children's Books
(a division of Abbey Home Media Group)

Abbey Home Media Group
435-437 Edgware Road
London W2 1TH
United Kingdom

Printed and bound by Dai Nippon, Hong Kong

Linking art to the world around us

artyfacts
Weather

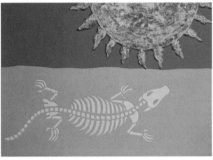

Contents

WRITTEN BY Janet Sacks

Weather watch

Have you ever sheltered in a doorway, knowing that the downpour will be over in a few minutes? Or looked at the sky to see whether it is cloudy or clear? If so, you are a weather forecaster, without realising it!

Cloud clues

People have always forecast the weather, even before they had scientific equipment to help them. Instead, they looked at weather patterns. Clouds give a clue to future weather. Thin, ripply cloud means good weather is on the way. Dark grey, low cloud is a sign of rain. The sky's colour is another clue: deep-blue means the air holds only a little water vapour, bright red means it holds a bit more, and pearly grey means that it contains a lot. If you get to know the weather patterns in your area, you'll be able to forecast the weather yourself!

Modern forecasts

Today, accurate weather forecasts are broadcast around the world, for up to five days ahead. Farmers listen to television or radio weather forecasts to help them decide when to plant or to harvest their crops. Pilots need to know what the local weather is like before landing their planes. Sailors at sea listen to shipping forecasts that mainly concentrate on winds.

Changing weather

Wherever you go on Earth, you can't get away from the weather. And no matter where you are, the weather is always changing. The biggest changes happen as the seasons move on through the year. Each season has its own weather – from hurricanes and monsoons to blizzards and drought.

Weather

WHAT YOU NEED

pencil

card

mounting card

glitter

brush

ruler

glue

paints

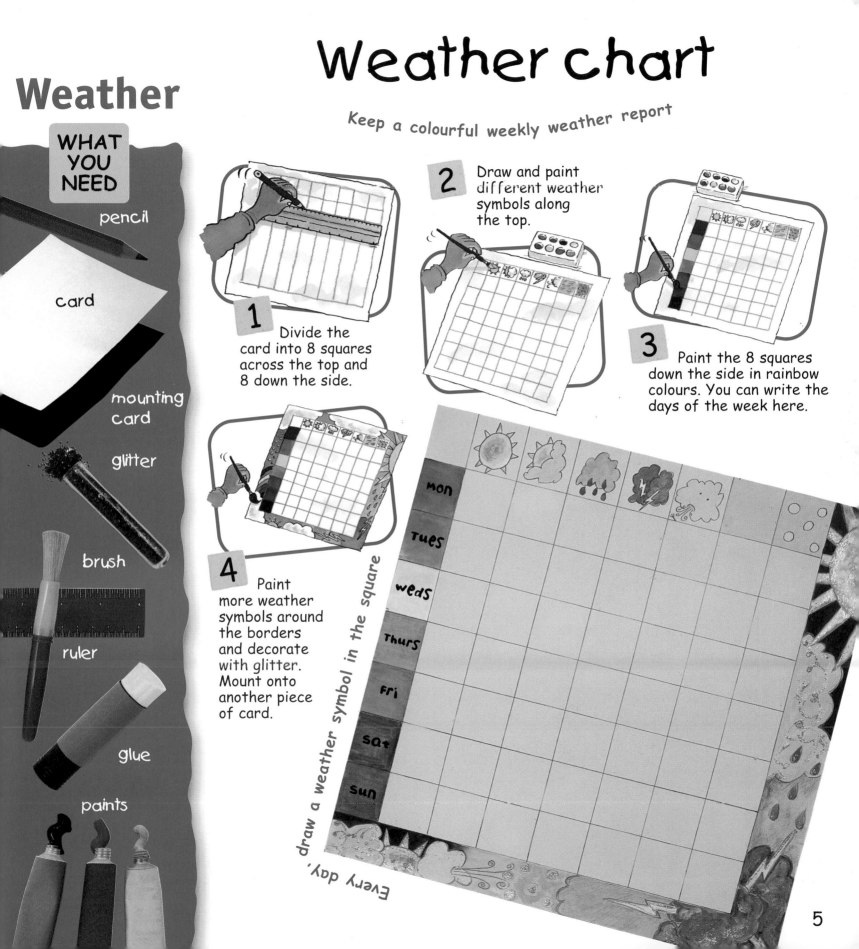

1 Divide the card into 8 squares across the top and 8 down the side.

2 Draw and paint different weather symbols along the top.

3 Paint the 8 squares down the side in rainbow colours. You can write the days of the week here.

4 Paint more weather symbols around the borders and decorate with glitter. Mount onto another piece of card.

mon
tues
weds
thurs
fri
sat
sun

Every day, draw a weather symbol in the square

Rainmakers

When you look up at the sky, you are likely to see the grey or white shapes of clouds. Sometimes, they are puffy white ones dotting the sky here and there. At other times, they cover the sky in a dull, grey sheet. There are many different types of clouds. They form in different types of weather.
If you look out of the same window every day for a week you will see several kinds. Four common cloud types are the fluffy cumulus, streaky cirrus, faint streaks of stratus, and the cumulonimbus storm clouds.

HOW CLOUDS ARE MADE

Clouds form and then disappear in a continual cycle as water rises into the air from the surface of the Earth and falls back down. When rain falls it collects in rivers, lakes and oceans. The heat of the Sun warms the water, which evaporates and rises as a gas called water vapour.

IT'S RAINING

As the water vapour rises higher into the atmosphere, the air pressure and temperature fall. This condenses, or changes, the water vapour into droplets which form clouds. The droplets may then begin to gather together around specks of dust carried by the wind. Gradually, the droplets get bigger. When they are too heavy to float in the air, they fall to the ground again as rain.

Fluffy cloud pictures

Create a storm and fill the sky with fabric and spatter clouds

WHAT YOU NEED

cotton wool

scissors

sponge

glue

coloured paper

toothbrush

pieces of fabric

white powder paint

1 Cut pieces of fabric into cloud shapes.

2 Glue them onto a piece of coloured paper.

3

Create different shapes from the cotton wool and add these to your fluffy cloud picture.

fabric clouds

spatter clouds

Spatter effect clouds

1 Mix some thick white powder paint.

2 Print different cloud shapes on coloured paper using the sponge dipped in paint.

3 Use the toothbrush to spatter paint and create light, see-through clouds.

7

Blowing winds

Wind is just air moving over the Earth. It may be a pleasant, gentle breeze, or strong enough to knock you flat. Some winds can be dangerous. A gale can whip up huge ocean waves that damage ships and flood land. A hurricane can destroy buildings and blow cars off the roads.

WEATHER CHANGER

The direction and strength of the wind affects our climate and weather. A wind blowing from a cool, dry area to a warmer, wetter area might cause the temperature and amount of moisture in the air to fall suddenly. Clouds, rain and even lightning may happen where the two masses of air meet. Later, a warm wind bringing warm air may cause showers and a rise in temperature.

HOT AIR, COLD AIR

Winds are created when the air around the Earth is heated unevenly by the Sun. The hotter air becomes lighter and rises. Cooler air then rushes in to take its place. The cooler air is then warmed, rises, and is replaced by another rush of cool air. Where this circulation of air happens most of the time, strong winds called prevailing winds blow. They include the trade winds that blow east to west across the oceans.

NAMING THE WIND

Most winds are known by the direction they blow from. But some have special names. The Mistral blows southwards in France. The Chinook blows westwards from the Rocky Mountains in Canada.

Spinning weathercock

WHAT YOU NEED

white card

scissors

wooden stick

pencil

cotton wool

foil

paints

paintbrush

glue

drinking straw

Can you see which way the wind is blowing?

1 Sketch the outline of a cockerel on the card. Cut it out and paint both sides.

2 Draw and cut out an arrow shape and cover it with foil.

3 Glue the arrow to the bottom of your cockerel.

4 Glue a straw to the bottom of the cockerel and plug the top end of the straw with cotton wool.

5 Place a stick inside the straw. Push the stick into the ground. Now the weathercock can spin in the wind!

9

Scattered showers

The water in a raindrop will have fallen to Earth many times before. Every day, the Sun dries up vast amounts of water from seas, lakes, rivers, plant leaves, puddles and even from your breath. The water rises into the air and forms clouds, then falls again as rain.

A RECYCLING CYCLE

The water cycle is a system that allows Earth's water to be used over and over again. This is how it works: first, the Sun's heat evaporates, or changes the water on Earth into a gas called water vapour. The water vapour collects together and floats higher and higher until it reaches cooler air. The coolness of the air changes the vapour from a gas back into tiny droplets of water, which join up to make a cloud.

RAIN OR DRIZZLE?

At first, the water droplets in the cloud are so small and light that they float. But as the air currents move them about, they join up into bigger, heavier drops. Finally, the drops fall. When a water droplet is more than 0.5 millimetres across, scientists call it rain. Smaller droplets falling close together are called drizzle. It is easy to tell rain from drizzle – when a raindrop falls into a puddle, it makes a splash!

MEASURING THE LEVEL

Scientists measure rain by catching the raindrops in a rain gauge. This has a scale on the side to measure the level of the water after one hour of rainfall. Less than 0.5 millimetres of rain is called 'light' rainfall. Medium rainfall is between 0.5 and 4 millimetres, and heavy rainfall is more than 4 millimetres.

RAINFALL ROUNDUP

It rains more in some parts of the world than in others. Britain has a climate that is neither very hot nor very cold. It has an average rainfall each year of between 62.5 and 250 centimetres. In a dry, hot desert the rain may hardly ever fall. And in warm, tropical countries, such as India, over 10,000 centimetres can fall in one year!

Weather

Drip paintings

WHAT YOU NEED

paper

paint

brush

mounting card

coloured acetate

sequins

glue

1 Water down some coloured paint and brush across the top of the paper.

2 Hold the paper upright and let the paint run down it.

Next time it rains have fun making rainy day pictures!

3 Draw and paint some people or animal shapes and cut them out.

4 Stick the shapes onto your picture and decorate with sequins.

PVA

5 Cut out umbrella shapes from the acetate and glue onto your picture.

11

White-out

Snowstorms can be fun. But heavy snow with high winds can also be frightening, and sometimes even dangerous. This kind of snowstorm is called a blizzard, and it often creates a 'white-out', in which all that can be seen is a vast curtain of white.

BLOWING BLIZZARDS

A blizzard occurs when a cold air mass from the Arctic region drifts south into the warmer, temperate regions of the world. When the two air masses meet, the colder, heavier air forces the warmer, lighter air to rise. This leads to a blizzard.

SWIRLING FLAKES

In a blizzard, snow falls heavily and the wind blows at up to 56 kilometres an hour. The temperature can drop down as far as –12°C. The distance you can see, called the range of visibility, is reduced to under 150 metres. In a severe blizzard, there may be winds of up to 72 kilometres an hour. At the same time, visibility can drop almost to zero, creating a total white-out.

SNOWDRIFT ZONES

Blizzards happen most often across the flat, northern plains of the USA, as well as in central Canada and parts of northern Asia. They can lead to heavy, drifting snow, causing major problems on roads and in towns.

Weather

Cover your window with pretty snowflake patterns

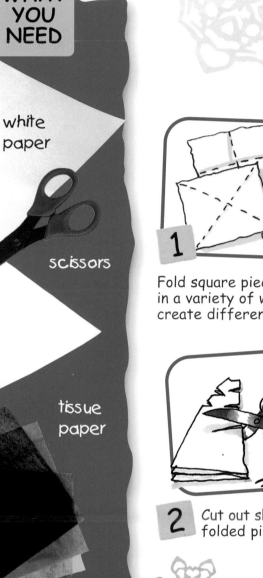

WHAT YOU NEED

white paper

scissors

tissue paper

glue

1 Fold square pieces of paper in a variety of ways to create different patterns.

2 Cut out shapes from each folded piece of paper.

3 Unfold each piece of paper and smooth them out flat.

4 Glue your snowflakes on to some tissue paper.

13

Thunderclap

Have you ever watched a thunderstorm from your window? It is exciting and scary at the same time! Lightning suddenly zig-zags across the sky with a huge flash. It is quickly followed by a deep, rumbling sound and a huge crash of thunder! But what causes it?

ELECTRIC CHARGE

Lightning happens when electricity builds up in a rain cloud. Each water drop in the cloud has a tiny charge of electricity. There are billions of water drops, so the whole cloud has a powerful charge of electricity. When the cloud comes close to either another cloud with an electric charge, or close to the ground, electricity rushes between them. The lightning flash we see is a huge electric spark. Each flash may be 30 kilometres long and last about 0.2 seconds!

LIGHTNING STRIKES

Lightning always finds the fastest way to the ground, usually through a tall tree or a building. It is very unusual for a person to be struck by lightning, but you should never shelter under a tree during a thunderstorm – if the height of the tree attracts the lightning, it will then switch to you!

THUNDER ROLL

Lightning heats up the air it flashes through, causing an explosion that sends out shock waves in all directions – it is these shockwaves that we hear as thunder.

Weather

Stormscape

Create a dramatic stormy picture with lightning flashes!

1 Glue on clouds made from cotton wool, scrunched up tissue paper and foil.

2 Paint all over with silver and sprinkle with glitter.

3 Glue glitter onto pipe cleaners. Shape them into lightning forks and stick onto the picture.

4 Paint on a landscape with trees. Decorate the leaves with glitter.

5 Mount on a piece of card.

Make your picture shine with silver and gold

Sky bridges

After it has rained, you sometimes see a beautiful rainbow arching across the sky. Long ago, people believed rainbows were magical and invented all kinds of stories about them. But the real magic of a many-coloured rainbow is that it is made of pure, white light!

WHITE LIGHT

White light is really a mixture of all the colours we see in a rainbow! Light travels in different size waves, called wavelengths. Each colour has a different wavelength. Red, for example, has a longer wavelength than violet.

BENDING SUNLIGHT

Light bends as it moves from thin air to thicker water, just as a straight stick in a glass of water looks partly bent. After the rain, the air is full of raindrops. They bend the sunlight, splitting it into colours to form a rainbow. White light can be split into different colours; these different colours can also be mixed up to make white again.

COLOUR COUNT

The colours that make white light are called the colours of the spectrum. In a rainbow, you'll always see these colours in the same order: red, orange, yellow, green, blue, indigo, violet. A second rainbow reverses the order so that violet is at the top.

Weather

WHAT YOU NEED

card

scissors

paints and brush

needle

pencil

ruler

elastic

Rainbow spinner

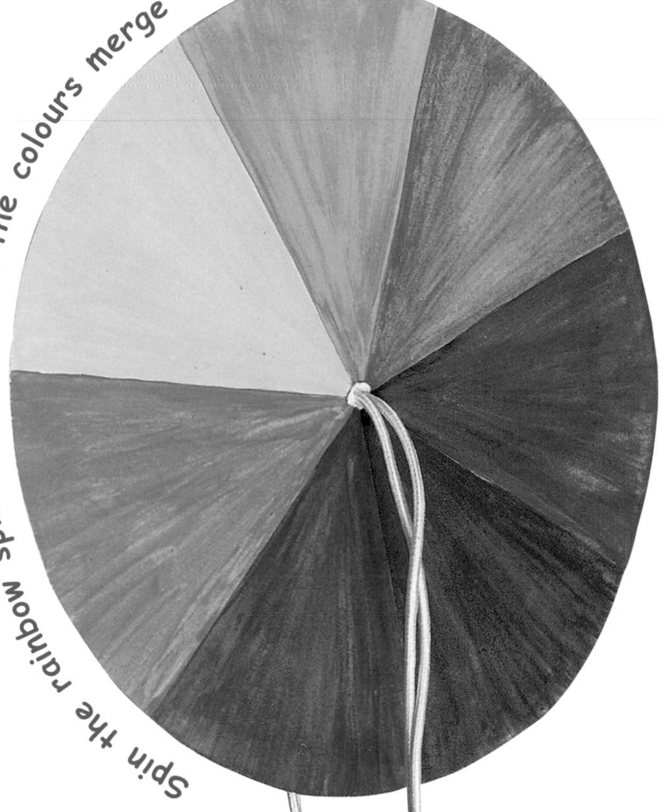

Spin the rainbow spinner and watch the colours merge to white!

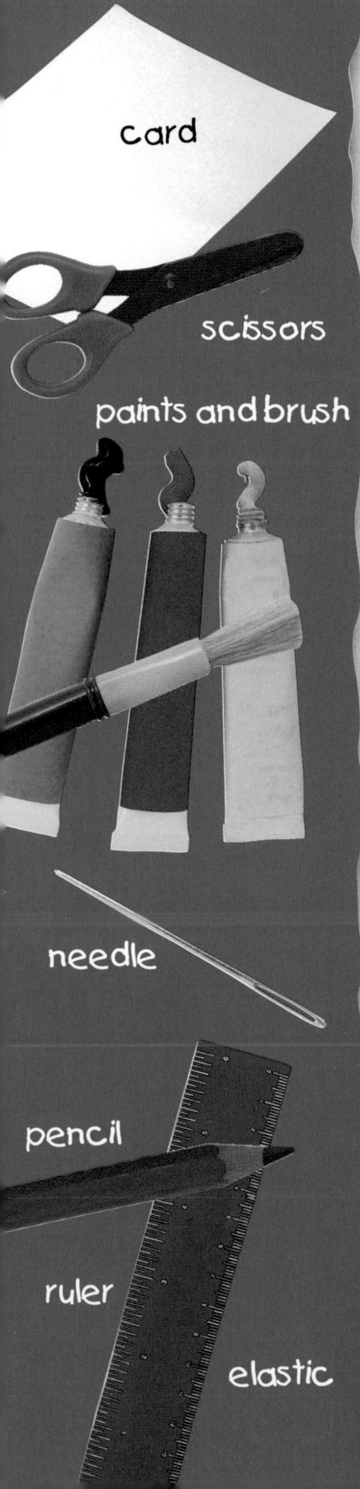

1 Draw a circle on the card and divide it into 7 sections.

2 Paint the 7 colours of the rainbow, one in each section.

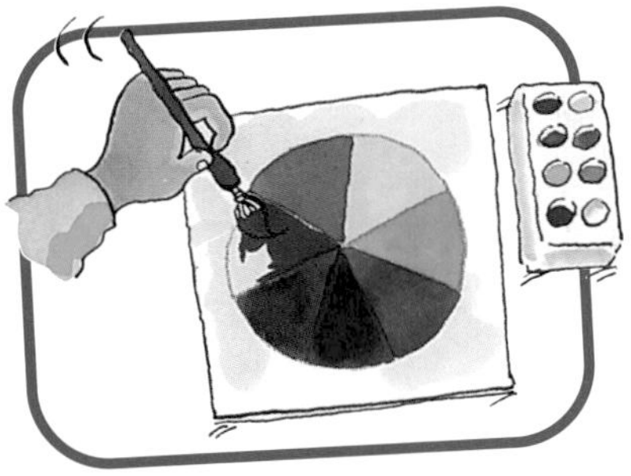

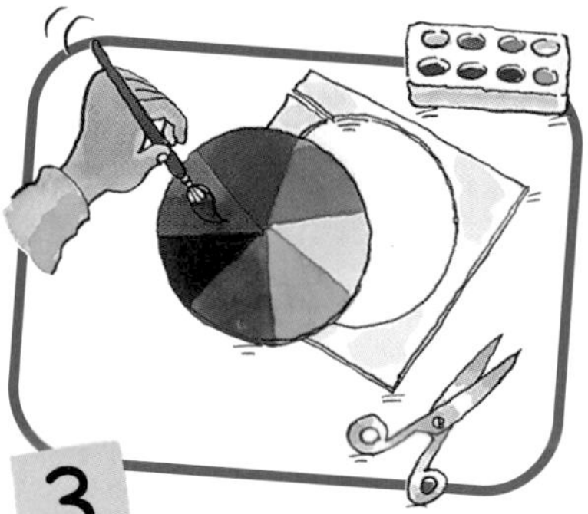

3 Cut the circle out and paint the other side exactly the same.

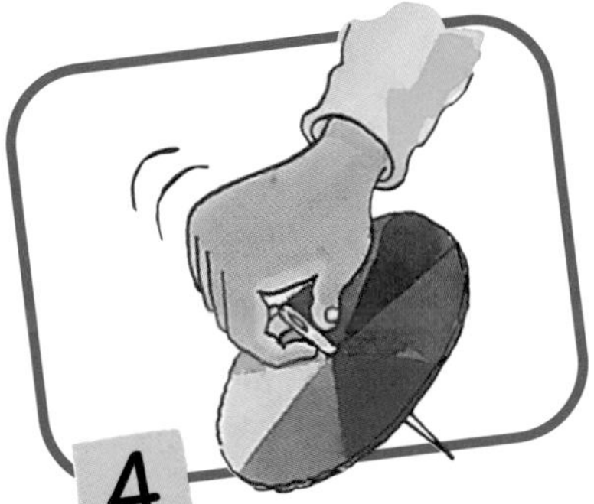

4 Make a hole in the middle.

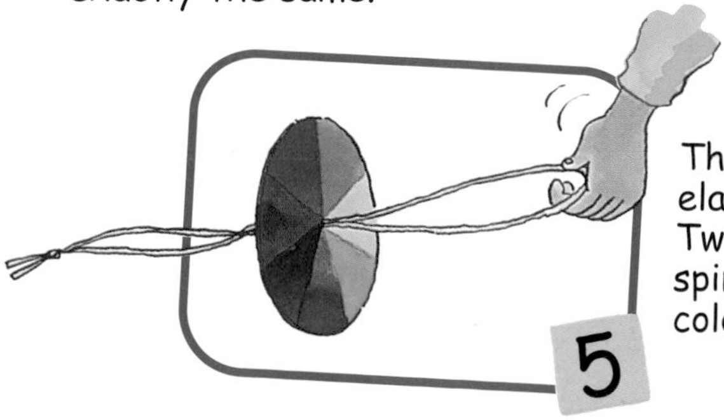

5 Thread a double piece of elastic through the centre. Twist it to make the circle spin fast. Now watch the colours blend into white.

Frosted patterns

Have you ever seen delicate crystal patterns on the windowpane in winter, or a covering of white on the grass? This is called frost and it happens when the outside temperature freezes, turning the water in the air to ice.

FREEZING FROST

After a freezing-cold night, soft, white ice crystals form on twigs, grass, and even on spiders' webs. This is called a hoar frost. Sometimes leaves are fringed with frozen fog droplets, called rime. The ice crystals reflect – or bounce – light in all directions, making the frost look white. But there is a black frost too. This is when water freezes in a sheet of hard, clear ice that is difficult to see.

ICE FROM THE SKY

Sometimes ice falls from the sky as frozen raindrops, called hail. They form in thunderstorms when they are swept up and down by wild air currents. The frozen raindrops collect several layers of ice until finally they fall. Sometimes hailstones are so big they are dangerous! In 1986, hailstones weighing 1 kilogram each killed 92 people in Bangladesh.

SIX-SIDED CRYSTALS

When a cloud reaches very cold air, the water vapour inside freezes into ice crystals that fall as snow. All snowflakes are six-sided, but each one is unique – no two have the same pattern!

Weather

WHAT YOU NEED

- silver paper or foil
- newspaper
- glitter
- glue
- sequins
- shells
- strips of bubble wrap
- twigs
- coloured card
- pebbles
- string

1 Stick strips of newspaper and bubble wrap across a sheet of silver paper or foil.

2 Glue small twigs, pebbles and shells onto the picture and decorate with glitter.

3 Glue string pieces to the sky as shown, and add sequins for snowflakes.

Mount onto card.

4

19

The big sleep

WINTER SLEEP

As cold weather approaches, food supplies fall. But when it is cold, animals need more food to stay warm and give them energy. One answer is to hibernate, or go to sleep. A hibernating mammal lowers its body temperature from around 32ºC to 4ºC. Its heart and breathing also slow right down. This way, the body uses hardly any energy to stay alive. For example, a hedgehog may only breathe once every six minutes! Animals get ready to hibernate by gorging on food in the autumn. When they wake again in spring, they may have lost nearly half their body weight.

HIDING PLACE

All hibernating creatures have to find a safe, warm place for their winter sleep. Many, such as mice, burrow underground, but bats hang upside down in hollow trees or a warm barn. Snails squeeze into cracks or under rocks, and seal the entrance to their shell with a thin skin called a membrane. Some creatures don't hide away for long — on mild days, squirrels and bears wake up and search for food.

A LONG, HOT SUMMER

In hot climates, some animals hibernate through the long, dry periods called droughts. Although male Californian ground squirrels sleep, the females must stay awake to look after their young. The African lungfish gorges itself on food during the rainy season. When the dry season comes, the fish burrows into mud, which dries round it like a protective cocoon.

As the weather turns colder and winter comes, some animals just seem to disappear. We don't see bats flitting about at night, or lizards scurrying around by day. That's because these animals are spending the winter asleep.

Weather

Hibernation box

Hibernation box

WHAT YOU NEED

- dried leaves
- newspaper
- tissue paper
- paint and brush
- hay
- cardboard box
- scissors
- glitter
- glue
- coloured card
- pencil
- paper

1 Cut a door shape in one panel of the box. Make a mound shape on top with scrunched-up newspaper, and fix with glue. Paint green or brown when dry.

2 Cut out leaf shapes from the tissue paper and stick all over the box. Add some real dry leaves. Put hay or grass inside.

Make a model hibernating animal to put into your box

Animal windows

Draw a tree landscape on a piece of paper. Paint and decorate with glitter. Cut out little window shapes amongst the leaves and trunks.

1

2 Draw and paint a series of hibernating animals and cut out.

3 Position the animals to line up with the holes you have cut. Then glue them onto coloured card. Now lie your nature scene on top.

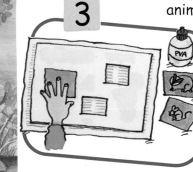

Turn the picture over, and open the windows of your nature scene

Weather machines

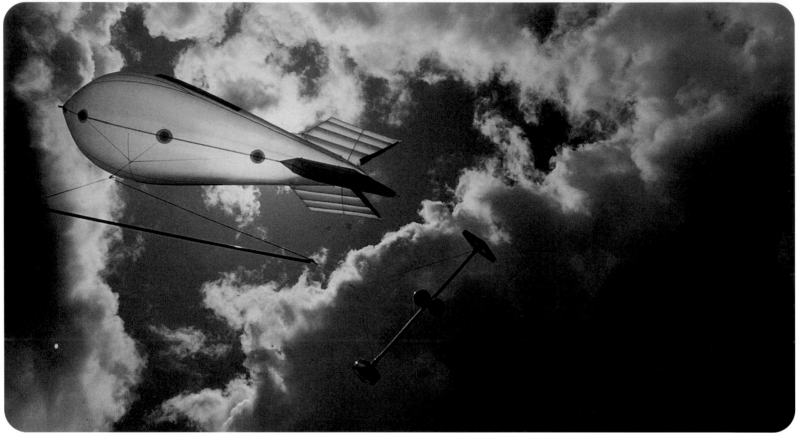

N o one knows exactly how hot, cold, or wet it will be tomorrow or next week. The weather can change so quickly, that even the experts get it wrong! To help them make their forecasts, scientists collect information with different weather instruments.

ON THE SURFACE

Some instruments gather information from near the Earth's surface. A barometer measures air pressure. 'High' usually means clear, sunny skies, 'low' means cloud or rain. An anemometer measures wind speed, a hygrometer measures the humidity, or amount of water in the air.

WEATHER BALLOONS

Every day, weather balloons are sent high into the air. They carry measuring instruments to record air temperature, humidity and wind speed. The information is sent back to weather stations on the ground.

SPACE SPIES

Weather satellites go up into space. They send back pictures of the weather around the world to computers on Earth. But the satellite pictures are not like pictures from an ordinary camera. One type measures the heat coming from the Earth's surface, the clouds, the oceans and the air, and shows them all as different colours.

Weather

WHAT YOU NEED

scissors

paint

brush

thick card

ping-pong ball

glue

string

pencil

button

glitter

metallic paint

Ping-pong hail ball

How many times can you bat the ball before you miss it?

Draw and cut out a bat shape from card.

1

2

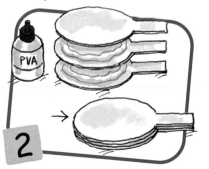

Repeat several times and stick at least 3 bat shapes together for strength. Paint and decorate with glitter.

3

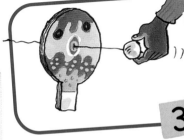

Thread string through the bat and attach to the ping-pong ball.

Barometer

1. Draw a thermometer shape on white card. Cut out.
2. Paint blocks of colour on the thermometer from blue at the bottom to red at the top.
3. Make a tab. Fold a small strip of card into two. Cut out 2 windows. Stick the ends together, leaving a gap so 1 window can slip over the thermometer.
4. Glue thermometer shape onto white card. Add silver-painted button. Decorate the card with weather symbols and colours, as shown.
5. Mount onto gold card. Cut a hole in the top so you can hang your barometer up.

very hot

hot

sunny

cloudy

rainy

freezing

Haloes and glories

AN ILLUSION

In hot weather, you can sometimes think you see pools of water on a dry road. This is an optical illusion, caused by bending light. The air close to the road heats up and spreads. Light entering this hot, thin air is bent. You see a brightness, which is actually a reflection of the sky above.

TRICK OF THE LIGHT

Sailors in polar regions have sometimes seen mountains floating on the sea! This is caused by colder, thicker air lying just above the sea's surface. It bends the light rays, to reflect images of mountains that are out of sight. Even stranger, the layer of warmer air above the cold air can twist the light rays – turning the mountains upside down! Whaling ships often first see one another as an upside-down picture in the sky!

GHOSTLY HALOES

When there is a lot of thin cloud in the sky, a ghostly white halo with a red rim can appear around the moon. It is formed in the same way as a rainbow, only the light is bent by ice crystals in the air, instead of raindrops.

GLORIES

Light can play tricks on us. Sometimes, it causes us to see things that aren't there. Some people have seen water in the desert and others have counted nine suns! This is because light bends as it travels through the sky.

When the clouds are low, it is possible to see the shadow of an aeroplane flying above them. The shadow may have rings of coloured light, called glories, all around it. Glories are caused when light enters the edge of tiny water droplets and bounces back. The light rays cross over, either destroying or joining with each other.

Weather

WHAT YOU NEED

white paper

glue

paint

brush

water

coloured card

Halo pictures

Use one, two or three colours in one picture

1 Cover the piece of paper with water.

Dot 'blobs' of colour on the wet surface and watch them spread out. **2**

3 When dry, mount your halo pictures on card.

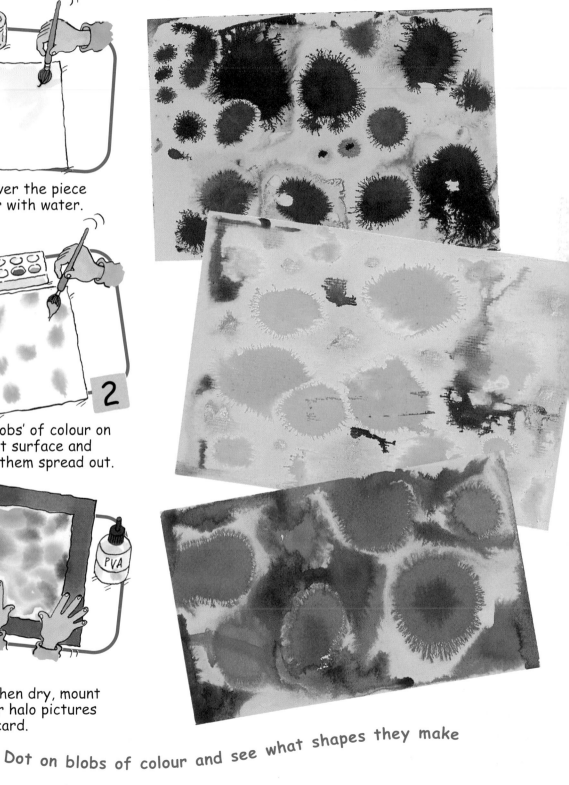

Dot on blobs of colour and see what shapes they make

25

Earth's blanket

T he atmosphere is the layer of gases around the Earth we call the air. It is like a blanket, keeping the world warm and protecting it from the Sun's more harmful rays. But the atmosphere is under attack – from pollution. Only we can stop the damage.

DANGEROUS HOLE

In the 1980s, scientists found a hole in the upper, ozone layer of the atmosphere. This layer stops the Sun's dangerous, ultraviolet rays reaching the Earth. It was being attacked by chemicals called CFCs, used in foam packing, refrigerators and aerosol sprays. Most countries have now banned CFCs, but the damage they have caused might last for many years.

THE GREENHOUSE EFFECT

The lower part of the atmosphere has the gases which keep heat close to the Earth. We call these gases 'greenhouse gases' because they work rather like the glass in a greenhouse. They let in light, but they don't let out all the Earth's heat. Without the greenhouse effect, the Earth would be cold and frozen. But pollution in the atmosphere has made the Earth heat up more than normal. Even a small rise in temperature can change the world's climate, leading to unusual weather, rising sea-levels and serious floods.

CARBON DIOXIDE

The main greenhouse gas is carbon dioxide. There is more in the atmosphere today than ever before. Carbon dioxide comes from car exhausts and from burning coal, gas and oil in power stations. It is also made when a rainforest is cleared by burning. To lower the carbon dioxide levels, we must burn less fossil fuel, clear fewer rainforests and use cleaner car fuel.

Weather

Mini greenhouse

WHAT YOU NEED

- cardboard box
- paper fasteners
- tissue paper
- scissors
- pipe cleaners
- clear acetate
- small plants
- paints
- paintbrush

1 Draw window and door frames on all four sides of the shoebox. Now draw windows and doors inside these frames. Shade them in so the framework is white.

2 Cut out the shaded windows and doors. Don't cut out the frames. Paint the framework and floor green.

3 Cut out two triangles of card. Measure the base of both triangles so they fit over the front and back walls of the greenhouse frame. Draw windows in each triangle and cut them out. Paint the frames and stick acetate on one side. Tape a triangle at each end of the main frame.

4 Fold another piece of card in half and cut it to size so that it opens out to make a roof. Cut out the windows, paint the frames and stick acetate on one side.

Make sure you water your greenhouse plants regularly. Plants need damp soil to grow.

Make climbing flowers from twisted pipe cleaners and tissue paper

27

Cracked earth

Imagine turning on the tap and no water running out. You can't have a drink when you feel thirsty, or a shower to get you clean. You might think this is okay – for a little while. But when a country runs out of water for a long time, the problems can be very serious.

NO RAIN

When rain that is expected doesn't come, it is called a drought. The drought might only last a short time, but sometimes a drought can last for months, or even years.

DRIED UP

A drought affects people's lives, because there isn't enough water for everything. When the water supply begins to be used up, it may have to be carefully rationed, or shared out. Farmers may not be able to water their crops, sheep and cattle may not have enough grass to eat because it has dried up, and fish may die when the water level in lakes and rivers goes down.

DEADLY DROUGHT

In 1968, a drought began in a narrow area of land called the Sahel, running right across Africa on the edge of the Sahara desert. In some parts, it is still going on. In 1983, drought hit Ethiopia in the north-east of Africa. The country soon ran out of food and thousands of people began to walk south. But when they reached the Sudan in the south, they faced more hunger when drought began there the next year.

Deadly desert scene

Picture the sun beating down on the dry desert sands

WHAT YOU NEED

yellow and blue card

white paint

brush

glue

pencil

white paper and card

scissors

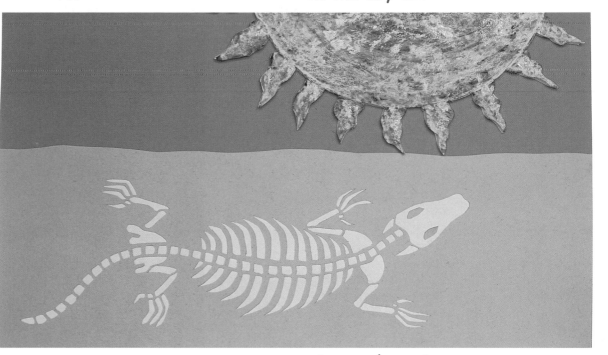

Create a split-level scene from coloured card

1 Using a very sharp pencil, draw a skeleton onto yellow card. You could trace over the picture above, or draw a shape of your own.

With white paint or pencil, colour in the individual bones of your skeleton very carefully. Then stick a sheet of blue card above the yellow card, as shown.

2

4 Glue the sun onto your desert picture.

3 Paint and decorate half a sun shape on thick card and cut out.

Green oasis

A desert is a dry, bare place where it hardly ever rains and where few plants can grow. But sometimes a green patch of land suddenly appears, full of growing plants and fresh water – an oasis!

HOT AND COLD

Deserts are so far away from the sea that the winds that blow there have lost their moisture. Most deserts are hot places, but there are some cold deserts. These are usually flat stretches of land high up in mountains. They are scorching hot in summer but freezing cold in winter.

MOUNTAIN WATER

An oasis appears where underground water comes to the surface. This water falls first as rain or snow on a faraway hill or mountain. It soaks into the ground and trickles through underground rocks to a low place in the desert. Then it flows up through a crack in the rock.

FERTILE LAND

With a supply of water all year, plants grow well on the desert soil. People have settled near large oases, and have even built cities. There they can grow wheat and fruit as well as clover to feed their sheep and camels.

Palm tree paradise

WHAT YOU NEED

- brown box lid
- tissue paper
- double-sided tape
- pencil
- sand
- scissors
- card
- glue
- green glitter
- paint and brush

1 Glue and sprinkle sand to cover the inside of the box lid. Cut out a circle of tissue paper and decorate with glitter to make a pool of water.

2 Draw the tops of palm trees and trunks on white card as shown. Paint and decorate with glitter. Cut out when dry.

3 Bring the 2 ends of the tree tops together. Attach with double-sided tape so they curve downwards.

4 Fold the trunks in half and tape together. Attach to the palms.

5 Draw bushes and grasses on card. Cut out and decorate.

6 Make slits so you can slot the pieces of grass and bushes together as shown. Glue everything to the base to complete your oasis.

Arrange all your plants around the pool in your shimmering oasis

Solar panels

The mirrors on this solar station are computer-controlled to track the path of the Sun.

W e call the heat and warmth from the Sun 'solar energy'. More of this free energy reaches us than can ever be made in the millions of power stations on Earth. Here are some of the ways we collect and use this amazing sunshine power.

HOT HOUSE

A solar house is a house heated by sunshine. It has special collectors, called solar panels, built on the roof or on the sunniest side of the house. Water flows through pipes inside the panels. During the day, this water is heated by the sunlight and pumped around the house.

HEAT MAKES POWER

In the hot Mojave desert in the USA, a curved mirror reflects sunlight on to a huge pipe filled with water. The water heats up and boils to make steam. The steam power turns a motor, called a turbine, to make electricity. In France, a solar furnace, or oven, is heated by hundreds of small mirrors reflecting sunlight onto one gigantic mirror. The Sun's energy is reflected off the gigantic mirror towards the furnace.

SOLAR CELLS

Solar cells are made of a material that makes electricity when light shines on it. Some cells work in ordinary indoor light, as well as natural sunlight. Many calculators and watches have solar cells. A group of large solar cells can make enough electricity for several homes, making solar power useful for small villages far from electricity supplies. There are even cars fitted with solar cells to power an electric motor.

Sun home

Weather

WHAT YOU NEED

cardboard box

glue

large sequins

scissors

bubble wrap

silver paint

foil

1 Paint the box silver.

2 Cut out square windows from bubble wrap and foil, and glue onto all four sides of the box.

3 Cut out a doorway from the front of the box, and glue on sequins.

4 Fold long rectangles of card into a 'V' shape with small panels on each side, as shown above. Paint silver. Glue the panels to the roof to complete your sun home.

You could make more buildings in different shapes, and add them to your display to create a sun city!

Place your sun home on the windowsill and feel the heat!

33

Weird weather

TOAD STORM

A tornado, or whirlwind, is a whirling funnel of wind. A really powerful tornado can spin so fast it can pick up a heavy truck, or uproot a tree. So a weaker wind, sweeping across a pond full of frogs, could easily lift them into the air, carry them along and then drop them far away. This was the explanation when a 'rainstorm' of toads fell over a town in Mexico in 1997!

RAINING FISH

A waterspout travelling across a lake or the sea can suck up the fish and dump them on the land. In Norway, a powerful waterspout once emptied a small harbour of all its fish – and all its water!

RAINBOW SNOW

A rainstorm sometimes leaves behind streaks of dirt or grains of sand. Sand from a faraway, warm desert can be carried thousands of miles by the wind. When the wind reaches a cooler place the sand falls to the ground in rain. Snow falling in the Alps mountains is sometimes coloured pink, red or brown by sand from the Sahara desert, 2,000 kilometres away!

DUCK FOR DINNER!

Some skyfalls really make you wonder! Try to explain these old stories: a downpour of huge, yellow mice; a heavy shower of black eggs; and a terrifying fall of live snakes! But the funniest fall of all was in 1973, in Arkansas, USA, when frozen ducks dropped out of the sky, giving everyone in the town a free duck dinner! Now, how do you think that happened?

Have you ever heard anyone say, 'It's raining cats and dogs!' when there is a downpour? It could never really rain cats or dogs – or could it? People have always told stories of skyfalls – when objects and animals fall from the sky.

Weather

It's raining frogs and fish

WHAT YOU NEED

- paper
- mounting card
- glue
- sequins
- glitter
- paint and brush
- pencil
- scissors
- white wax crayon

1 Rub the wax crayon all over the paper, then add a wash of blue paint on top.

2 Draw and paint lots of different fish and frogs on a separate piece of paper.

3 Cut out the shapes and stick them onto the waxed paper.

Wax and paint mix to produce an excellent 'water' effect

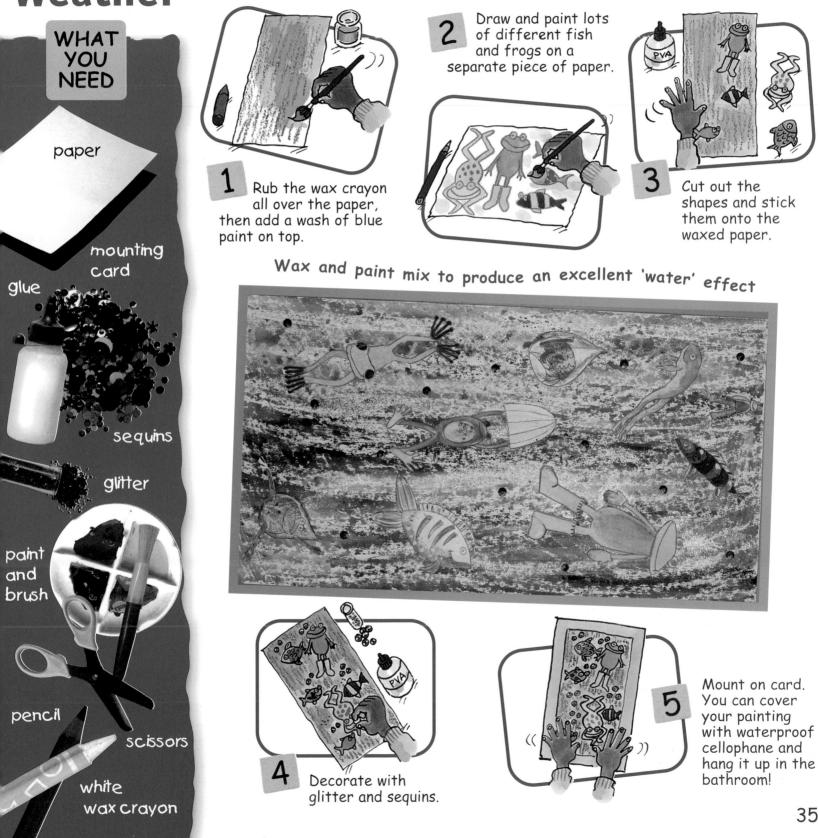

4 Decorate with glitter and sequins.

5 Mount on card. You can cover your painting with waterproof cellophane and hang it up in the bathroom!

35

Washed up

*A*ll around the world, people have built towns and villages by rivers. It is a good place to choose – the river supplies water for homes, farms and factories. And the river can carry people and goods from place to place. However, there is just one problem – flooding.

AN OVERFLOW

A flood happens when a river swells with too much water. If nothing stops it, a river can burst its banks and send water rushing into homes, businesses, and across farmers' fields. The Yangtze river in China has flooded out of control like this, time after time. But for thousands of years, farmers in Egypt welcomed the yearly Nile river floods because they fertilised the soil.

RAIN AND ICE

A flood can happen when a lot of rain falls in a short time, so that rivers burst their banks. In India, when winds full of moisture blow onto the land, they bring heavy rain and flooding which can last for months. This is called the monsoon. In central Europe, the Danube river has often flooded in spring, when ice breaks away from its banks and piles up, causing an overflow.

FLOOD CONTROL

There are, however, ways to slow down or even stop flooding. River banks can be built up with earth, rock or concrete. A concrete dam can hold back the water's flow, and a barrier across a river can be lowered to change the speed of the flow.

Weather

WHAT YOU NEED

- card
- sequins
- glue
- scissors
- brush
- paint
- varnish
- elastic
- pencil
- tape
- tissue paper

Rainhat

1 Cut out a circle from the card. Then cut a line from the edge to the middle.

2 Overlap the edges into a cone shape and glue.

3 Paint and decorate. Tape a piece of elastic to go under the chin. Varnish to waterproof.

Sunhat

1 Draw and cut a circle from the card, and cut out a smaller circle inside the big one.

2 Paint and decorate with sequins to complete the brim of your hat.

3 Place tissue paper through the inner circle to create the top of the hat and glue into place. Attach a piece of elastic as before.

37

Acid rain

Splashing in the rain can be fun! But did you know that a certain kind of rain is dangerous? This is acid rain. It can poison water, plants and animals, and even damage stone buildings.

POLLUTION

Acid rain is a type of pollution. It comes from harmful gases caused by burning fossil fuels, such as coal, gas and oil. When the gases rise into the air, they mix with sunlight and water in the clouds, turning them acid. The acid then falls as rain.

ACID DAMAGE

Acid rain is more acid than vinegar, so it causes serious damage to buildings. The Parthenon and the Taj Mahal are two world-famous buildings, slowly being dissolved by acid rain. It has destroyed huge areas of forests in Germany, and thousands of lakes in Sweden and the USA are so acid that the fish in them have died. The wind can blow acid rain clouds from one country to another; for example, pollution from industry in Britain has been carried to Norway and Sweden.

COUNT THE COST

Industries say that cleaning up the gases that cause acid rain would cost them too much money. We burn fossil fuels to make electricity, but electricity can also be made from cleaner fuels, such as nuclear energy, water, wind and solar power. A clean-up of fuel will only happen if governments insist upon it.

Weather

Blow painting

paper

paint brush

glue

straw

mounting card

ink

1 Place blobs of ink at the bottom of a piece of paper.

Blow the ink upwards using your straw.

2

3 Mount the picture onto card when it's dry.

You can create dramatic shapes with this technique

See how the lines look like dead trees

Spinning storms

A hurricane is a great, boiling circle of wind and rain. It can blow as hard as 322 kilometres an hour! Tornadoes, or twisters, are only one hundredth as big as a hurricane. But as they blow across the land, they can tear up big trees by the roots and push over whole buildings.

SUPER STORM

Hurricanes start over tropical oceans. As great masses of warm, wet air rise up, towering rain clouds form and begin to whirl. In the middle the air is perfectly calm. This spot is called the eye of the hurricane. The spinning winds suck up huge amounts of water vapour which later fall as torrential rain. Storms like this are also called typhoons or cyclones.

AIR RUSH

A tornado looks like a huge, twisting snake hanging down from a cloud. Tornadoes start over the land when warm, moist air is underneath cold, dry air. As the warm air rises, it quickly cools, making hail and rain fall. Air rushes in from all around to take the place of the rising warm air, and begins to whirl. A tornado can blow as hard as a hurricane. As it travels across the ground, it makes a roaring sound. Powerful tornadoes can pick up everything in their path – people, animals, trucks, even trains and bridges!

Weather

Dizzy twister

WHAT YOU NEED

black paint

plastic bottle

newspaper

tape

wire and cable

bubble wrap

glue

white tissue paper

sequins

silver paint

bottle tops

1 Roll and twist lengths of newpaper and tape around the plastic bottle in a spiral shape.

2 Cover the whole of the structure with papier mâché, and finish off with a layer of white tissue paper. Leave to dry.

3 When it is dry, paint it black and then wrap and twist pieces of wire and cable around the twister.

4 Thread bottle tops with wire, and hang from the twisted cable. Attach sequins all over, and paint silver blobs at intervals to catch the light.

Twisting, turning, spinning, shimmering. Amazing!

Turn your tornado round and round and listen to the whistling, clanking sound it makes. Just like the real thing!

Thick fog

Walking in a fog is like walking through a cloud. Sometimes a fog is so thick that you can't see very far ahead of you. At other times, it is like a misty veil. How thick or thin a fog is depends on how cold the air is, and how much water it can hold.

Smoky fog

Fog is caused when water vapour in the air condenses, or changes into minute droplets of water, rather like a cloud. If the water vapour condenses around dust and smoke particles, it is called 'smog'. Smog happens in industrial places, where chimneys belch chemicals, such as sulphur, into the air. Smog can affect people's eyes and breathing. It usually happens when there is no wind to blow it away.

Sea fog

When a fog horn booms out in the night, it is warning other ships of coastal fog. Sea fogs happen in late spring, before the sea has a chance to warm up. When the wind carries warm, moist air over a cold sea, the warm air cools and condenses, causing a fog. The worst sea fogs happen near Newfoundland, Canada, where cool, foggy air wraps itself around icebergs and makes them an invisible danger to ships!

Dew drops

Have you ever looked out in the morning and seen twigs and spiders' webs glistening with dewdrops? This happens after a clear, still, autumn night, when the ground loses heat quickly and there are no clouds to trap any warm air.

Weather

WHAT YOU NEED

black and white card

paint

pencil

brush

gluestick

toothbrush

white paint

Foggy landscape

1 Draw and paint a landscape onto the black card.

Use the toothbrush to flick white paint onto the picture to look like fog.

2

3 Use your pencil to dot texture onto the picture.

4 Mount on white card.

Flick colour on top of your picture to create a misty effect

Fly away home

When autumn comes, flocks of birds, such as geese, gather together and fly away. Have you ever wondered where they are flying to? And, even more puzzling, how the birds will find their way?

MORE FOOD

Birds fly away, or migrate from one country to another when the seasons change. They need a lot of food to keep warm and this is harder to find when it gets colder. And as the days grow shorter, the birds have less time to search for food. So they fly south to somewhere warmer, where there is plenty to eat.

MAGNETIC FORCE

How birds find their way, or navigate is a puzzle. Some birds may follow the invisible magnetic force lines around the Earth. Others navigate by watching the position of the Sun. Night birds navigate by the position of certain stars.

FINDING THE WAY

A bird's homing instinct is extraordinary. Scientists moved a bird called a Manx shearwater 5,000 kilometres from its nest, and set it free. Twelve days later it had flown back home!

LONG-DISTANCE BUTTERFLIES

The monarch butterfly has one of the longest of all insect migrations. Monarchs spend the winter in mass roosts on trees in warm California or near Mexico City. In spring, they migrate north – some even reach Canada by late summer. Then they return south for the winter.

Weather

Butterfly tree

How many butterflies can you stick on your tree?

WHAT YOU NEED

paper

mounting card

pencil

glue

scissors

tissue paper

card

sequins

black paint

brush

paint

1 Draw an outline of a tree on the card, paint and cut out.

2 Cut out leaf shapes from coloured tissue paper and stick to the branches of the tree.

3 Draw and cut out butterfly shapes from paper. Paint and decorate with sequins. Stick on the tree.

4 Cut a triangular shape from card as shown and stick to the back of the tree to stand it upright.

Birds on wire

Draw an outline of birds sitting on a wire. Paint them black. Mount on card.

Glossary and Index

acid rain 38

air current A moving flow of air. 18

air pressure The pushing force of air. 6, 22

anemometer An instrument used to measure how fast the wind is blowing. 22

Arctic region The area around the North Pole where the land and sea are covered with ice. 12

atmosphere The mixture of gases surrounding the Earth that we call air. 6, 26

barometer An instrument that measures air pressure, used to forecast the weather. 22

blizzard A severe snowstorm with fiercely blowing winds. 12

carbon dioxide 26

CFCs Chemicals that attack the ozone layer, found in some packing material, and aerosol sprays. They have now been banned. 26

Chinook A wind that blows in the Rocky Mountains of Canada. 8

cirrus A streaky cloud that promises dry weather. 6

climate The usual pattern of weather in an area. 8

cloud Billions of tiny, floating water droplets gathered together in the sky. 4, 6, 8, 14, 22, 24, 42

crystal 18

cumulonimbus Heavy storm clouds. 6

cumulus A large fluffy cloud which promises warm windy weather. 6

cyclone 40

dam 36

desert 28, 30, 34

dew 42

drought A time when no rain falls and wells, rivers, lakes and reservoirs dry up. 28

electric charge The electricity in something, such as a water droplet in a cloud. 14

evaporate To change from a liquid, such as water, into an invisible, floating gas. 6, 10

fog Water vapour in the air that has changed into tiny water droplets. 18, 42

frost Water droplets in the air that have frozen into ice crystals. 18

gale A very strong wind that blows at more than 51 kilometres an hour. 8

greenhouse effect 26

hail Frozen raindrops made from ice layers, called hail stones, falling from the sky. 18

halo A thin white light around the rim of the Moon. 24

hibernate 20

hoar frost 18

humidity The amount of water, or moisture, that is in the air. 22

hurricane 8, 40

hygrometer 22

ice 18, 36

light waves Invisible, flowing streams of light, also called light rays. 16, 24

lightning A flash of bright light that happens during a thunderstorm. 8, 14

magnetism 44

migrate 44

Mistral A wind that blows southwards in France. 8

monsoon 36

nuclear energy 38

oasis 30

optical illusion A trick of the light that fools your eye into seeing an image that is not actually there. 24

ozone layer The high layer of the atmosphere which protects Earth from the Sun's harmful ulraviolet rays. 26

pollution 26, 38

power station A place where different kinds of energy or fuel are used to make electricity, or another form of power. 32

prevailing wind A certain wind that blows all the time, such as the trade winds that blow east to west across the Earth. 8

rain Droplets in a cloud which have grown too heavy to float in the air and so fall to the ground. 6, 8, 10, 20, 22, 28, 34, 38, 40

rainbow The arc of colours you see in the sky, caused when raindrops split sunlight into the seven colours of the spectrum. 16

reflection The image you see when the light waves from an object bounce off another surface before coming into your eyes. 24

shipping forecast 4

smog Fog formed from water vapour, dust and smoke particles. 42

snow Ice crystals that form inside clouds from water vapour and fall to the ground. 12, 18

snowflake 13, 18

snowstorm Snowy weather that is also very windy. 12

solar cells The light-collecting parts of machines, such as a calculator or a car, which work using solar energy. 32

solar energy The Sun's heat and light, which can be used to make energy, such as electricity. 32, 38

solar panels Flat panels specially designed to collect the heat from the Sun. 32

spectrum The seven colours of light we can see: red, orange, yellow, green, blue, indigo, violet. 16

stratus High streaky cloud. 6

Sun The star around which the Earth orbits, or turns, and which sends us warmth and light. 6, 8, 10, 32, 44

temperature How warm or cold the air is, measured in degrees. 6, 8, 12, 18

thunder The booming sound you hear during a thunderstorm. It is a shockwave, caused by lightning heating up the air very fast. 14

thunderstorm A storm where thunder and lightning happen, caused by a build up of electricity in the clouds. 14

tornado 34, 40

turbine A machine turned by energy, such as wind, or solar power. As it spins, it turns a generator, to make electricity. 32

twister 40

typhoon 40

ultraviolet ray 26

visibility How far ahead you can see in snowy, rainy, or foggy weather. 12

water cycle The way in which water moves around the Earth. It evaporates from seas and rivers, rises into the air to form clouds, then falls back to Earth again as rain. 6, 10

waterspout 34

water vapour The invisible gas that forms when water warms up and evaporates. 6, 18, 40, 42

wavelength 16

weather balloon An air balloon that is sent into the atmosphere to measure temperature, humidity and wind speed. 22

weather forecast A description of the weather to come, usually made by a scientist called a weather forecaster. 4, 22

weather satellite A space satellite that sends pictures of weather around the world to computers on Earth. 22

weather station A place where information from weather balloons and satellites is received by computers, and used to forecast the weather. 22

whirlwind 34

white light Ordinary daylight made of the seven colours of the spectrum, but which looks as if it has no colour at all. 16

white-out When there is so much snow, that you cannot see anything ahead, only whiteness. 12

wind Air that is moving around the Earth. 8, 22, 34, 36, 38, 40